Healing from Narcissism

The handbook for surviving in a narcissistic relationship. Develop your personality to help the narcissist recover from personality disorder.

Kevin Roberts

Table of Contents

Furthermore, the transmission, duplication, or reproduction of any of the following work including specific information will be considered an illegal act irrespective of if it is done electronically or in print. This extends to creating a secondary or tertiary copy of the work or a recorded copy and is only allowed with the express written consent from the Publisher. All additional right reserved.

The information in the following pages is broadly considered a truthful and accurate account of facts and as such, any inattention, use, or misuse of the information in question by the reader will render any resulting actions solely under their purview. There are no scenarios in which the publisher or the original author of this work can be in any fashion deemed liable for any hardship or damages that may befall them after undertaking information described herein.

Additionally, the information in the following pages is intended only for informational purposes and should thus be thought of as universal. As befitting its nature, it is presented without assurance regarding its prolonged validity or interim quality. Trademarks that are mentioned are done without written consent and can in no way be considered an endorsement from the trademark holder.

EMPATH AND ENERGY VAMPIRES

Have you at any point had a companion or relative who left you sincerely depleted? Possibly they possibly called you when they expected to vent, or they were strong one day and ultra-basic the following. Or then again maybe they wore you out physically—to the point that you expected to clock some genuine self-care time in the wake of spending time with them.

If thus, you've likely had a run in with what a few specialists call a "vitality vampire." This hungry-for-consideration character type is continually searching for somebody's essentialness to deplete. Furthermore, if you're exceptionally delicate and will in general interpretation of the feelings of others—AKA an empath—you're an ideal objective.

"All people emanate vitality, however empaths transmit a specific kind of empathetic and understanding vitality that can go about as a heavenly life blood for vitality vampires," composes Christiane Northrup, MD, in her new book, Dodging Energy Vampires. "[Empaths] don't have a clue where they end and another starts." They likewise want to help— many work in mending callings—which leaves them defenseless to the determined controls of vitality vampires.

Yet, how would you know if you're an empath? As indicated by Dr. Northrup, the most widely recognized signs are "uncommon affectability to sound, to smells, to swarms, [and] to brutality." And when looked with a vampire, your body will probably tell you. (Dr. Northrup, herself an empath, reviews a period she was so contrarily influenced by a vitality vampire's essence that she needed to race to the washroom to upchuck.)

While the most sure-fire path for empaths to secure themselves is to cut off all ties, that isn't constantly a practical arrangement—maybe your vitality vampire is an associate or a nearby relative. In those cases, Dr. Northrup prescribes a three-advance way to deal with seal up your own "vitality releases," no garlic required.

Continue perusing to figure out how to shield yourself from individuals who channel your vitality.

Vitality vampires and how to fend them off

Become exhausting

The vitality vampire's fuel—what Dr. Northrup calls the "narcissistic stockpile"— is the enthusiastic lift they stand out enough to be noticed. By displaying the least-fascinating rendition of yourself, they don't have anything to draw upon. "The vitality vampire will overlook you and go to another person," clarifies Dr. Northrup. What's more, don't stress over disliking you for being dull or hesitant. Your genuine companions will comprehend, Northrup says.

Figure out how to state no

Empaths need to battle the drive to consistently be accessible, for the wellbeing of self-preservation. Be that as it may, it's more difficult than one might expect. "Saying 'no' quickly is a PhD-level ability," says Dr. Northrup. "So what you do rather is you state, 'Let me hit you up.'" That basic expression will give you the time you have to choose whether you can (or should) associate with that individual, she says, and in the long run assist you with getting to "no."

Affirm the vampire's aim

Significantly subsequent to rehearsing your "let me hit you up" and your "sorry, however no," you may in any case feel constrained to yield to a vitality vampire's needs or needs. In any case, before you state "yes" to any favors, ask a believed companion what they think. Odds are, they'll recognize the truth about the circumstance: the vitality vampire's chance to lay into you by and by.

To the exclusion of everything else, says Dr. Northrup, recollect that you're not the only one and your empathic characteristics are a quality, not a shortcoming. "What occurs with most empaths is that we believe we're insane because we've never been approved," she says. "Nothing isn't right with you." You're simply somebody who needs to take the expression "great vibes just" extra truly.

Passionate vampire is a casual term for dangerous individuals who channel us of our vitality and leave us feeling genuinely depleted. They have a parasitic quality in that they incite passionate responses in others and "feed off" their feelings just as assets. Empaths and exceptionally delicate individuals will in general be focused by passionate vampires because of the quality of their feelings and lively vitality.

We've all heard the expression "enthusiastic vampire," however what does it truly mean? I consider "passionate vampire" to be a casual term for harmful individuals who deny us of our vitality, our feeling of enthusiastic wellbeing and our capacity to take part in self-care. Being around a passionate vampire can make us feel discouraged, on edge, scared, confounded and in torment. It can influence our efficiency, our capacity to center and our general mental, physical and passionate prosperity.

This term is generally used to portray narcissists and sociopaths who mentally drain us dry. It can likewise be applied to commonplace harmful individuals who are conceited and self-ingested. Whatever point at the range the passionate vampire falls upon, in any case, the person can negatively affect your emotional wellbeing.

Empaths and profoundly delicate individuals may be particularly powerless to being around these sorts because enthusiastic vampires are attracted to our glow, our sympathy and our splendid vitality. Passionate vampires devour these characteristics to satisfy themselves while leaving you feeling debilitated and depleted.

There are seven signs you should keep an eye out for if you trust you may be managing a passionate vampire.

1. They drain you physically and sincerely so you can't like yourself or be gainful.

Being around a poisonous individual resembles being overloaded by substantial dark tar. It can influence you on both a mental and physiological level. You feel immobilized. Your entire body can respond: perhaps your heart thumps quicker, your palms sweat, and you get a throbbing feeling of something not being directly in your gut or heart. You may encounter torment or physical illnesses that appear unexpectedly.

Mentally, you feel a lessened feeling of organization and an expanded feeling of sadness. You can't respond usefully because this poisonous individual's inordinate qualification, absence of empathy and explicit negligence for your feelings saturates each communication you have with them. They channel your vitality with the goal that you're never again ready to put your full spotlight on the things that genuinely matter.

They will likely occupy you with their manipulative strategies so you're never again serving your most noteworthy great – rather, you're taking into account their inner self, solely serving them and their needs.

2. When you're no longer in their quality, you may in any case feel influenced by them.

You end up ruminating over peculiar things they said or unfeeling things they did to you. You're probably going to feel sincerely depleted by their jokes, their endeavors to begin show or their glaring disregard of your fundamental needs and rights. You wind up scrutinizing your very own existence and being tormented with a persevering feeling of self-question.

Serious nervousness is regular for empaths who've been "contacted" by the effect of an enthusiastic vampire. Gloom is often inescapable symptom of being encompassed by passionate vampires for significant stretches of time.

3. You begin to feel lively after you are away from them for a couple of days or half a month, anyway long it takes you to completely "detox" from them.

When you've expelled yourself from the poisonous individual and have had the opportunity to mentally "reset," you feel a lot lighter, more joyful and increasingly profitable. It's as though an extraordinary weight has been lifted and you're presently ready to push ahead into more prominent lucidity and restored quality. In any case, if you ever cooperate with them again, you may get yourself again cleared away by their crazymaking turmoil.

4. Indeed, even a basic discussion with them over something that ought to have a straightforward arrangement leaves you feeling bewildered and confounded.

You wind up clarifying fundamental human goodness, decency, and honesty to them again and again. They will not offer you straight responses and they won't respect you as an individual who merits thought and regard. They anticipate their dangerous qualities onto you, they become excessively guarded about their uncalled for conduct, and they are indifferent to the torment you might be encountering because of their disregard or misuse.

5. They're similar to a needle to an inflatable and their parasitic nature can make you have a feeling that you're getting poisonous, as well.

Enthusiastic vampires benefit from your positive vitality while leaving you malnourished. When you're feeling upbeat, confident and sure, they attempt to come around to "collapse" you with put-downs, analysis or a mischievous strategy to disrupt or undermine you.

Strikingly, similarly as legendary vampires can "chomp" their exploited people and transform them into vampires, I find that the more you're around a passionate vampire, the more you begin to get on a portion of their dangerous propensities and enthusiastic states.

For unfortunate casualties who've been threatened by narcissists, we call this getting "narcissistic bugs." It's a brief condition of taking on a portion of the dangerous attributes you've been presented to. That is the reason it's so critical to get as far away as you can, particularly if you're an empath who disguises the feelings of others like a wipe. The exact opposite thing you need is to turn out to be so poisonous yourself because of these sorts that you overlook where the predator starts and you end.

6. There is nothing of the sort as correspondence with them; you are here to satisfy their needs while they disregard yours.

Passionate vampires are uneven. That implies whenever you're too much providing for them (as empaths are probably going to do), they're cheering in taking from you. Their discussions will typically focus them and highlight them as the unparalleled individual who is significant. They settle on choices that influence you while never thinking about how you would feel about them. They micromanage and control you to make themselves feel prevalent and incredible. They are the end-all, be-all of everything.

EMPATH AND SPIRITUAL HYPERSENSITIVITY

As a therapist and an empath, I often get asked, "What is the difference among empaths and profoundly delicate individuals?" In The Empath's Survival Guide I dedicate an area on this significant differentiation.

Here are the likenesses and differences. Empaths share every one of the attributes of what Dr. Elaine Aron has called "Profoundly Sensitive People," or HSPs. These incorporate a low edge for incitement, the requirement for alone time, affectability to light, stable, and smell, in addition to an abhorrence for enormous gatherings.

It additionally takes profoundly touchy individuals longer to slow down following a bustling day since their framework's capacity to progress from high incitement to hushing up is more slow. Profoundly delicate individuals are regularly thoughtful people while empaths can be self-observers or outgoing individuals, (however most are contemplative people). Empaths share a profoundly touchy individual's affection for nature, calm conditions, want to help other people, and a rich internal life.

Be that as it may, empaths take the experience of the exceptionally touchy individual a lot further. We can detect unpretentious vitality, which is called shakti or prana in Eastern recuperating customs, and really retain it from others and different situations into our own bodies. Profoundly touchy individuals don't commonly do that.

This limit enables us to encounter the energies around us in amazingly profound manners. Since everything is made of inconspicuous vitality, including feelings and physical sensations, we vivaciously disguise the sentiments and torment of others. We often experience difficulty recognizing another person's inconvenience from our own. Additionally, some empaths have significant otherworldly and instinctive encounters which aren't normally connected with profoundly delicate individuals. Some can speak with creatures, nature, and their internal aides. In my book there is a segment on natural empaths which incorporate creature empaths, earth empaths, dream empaths, clairvoyant empaths and the sky is the limit from there.

Being a profoundly touchy individual and an empath are not fundamentally unrelated: you can be both simultaneously. Numerous exceptionally delicate individuals are likewise empaths.

If you consider this differentiation as far as an empathic range, empaths are on the best quality; profoundly delicate individuals are a little lower on the range, individuals with solid empathy yet who are not HSPs or empaths are in the range. Narcissists, sociopaths and mental cases who have "empath lacking issue" are at the least finish of the range.

The gifts of affectability and empathy are valuable, particularly during this season of human development. We need to continue opening our hearts and leap forward to new highs in the empathic range. I offer the strategies in my book on empaths with the goal that turning out to be engaged empaths and profoundly delicate individuals can occur at quickened rates in our reality. We need your gifts like never before!

SPIRITUAL PURPOSE OF EMPATH

One of the most as often as possible posed inquiries by those on the way of enlivening is: What is my motivation in life?

I realize very well indeed that it is so baffling to have this inquiry consuming unanswered inside.

For the Empath it is doubly disappointing because we have this unfathomable gift and most don't have a clue what it is really going after what we should do with it.

I have often been posed inquiries, for example, 'how might I be of administration to other people?' or 'I need to help other people yet by what method would it be advisable for me to do it?'

It is an innate attribute for Empaths to need to help other people, particularly if they are enduring. Nonetheless, huge numbers of us have attempted and bombed when endeavoring to help other people help themselves.

It very well may be unimaginably soul-crushing to see another affliction and not have the option to support them.

I have come to comprehend that not all enduring is a terrible thing. It is through enduring that people start to develop, stir and start searching for another, better way in life. Enduring can likewise be a significant transitional experience into profound awareness.

A considerable lot of us feel like we are enduring when we don't have the foggiest idea about our motivation in life.

We as a whole need heading and reason, regardless of how advanced we are. Furthermore, it is up to every one of us to search out that bearing for our self. So as to fill their life need, numerous Empaths accept they ought to be working straightforwardly with others. Be that as it may, for some, this simply isn't a choice because of the getting 'inhabited' factor.

In all actuality, Empaths don't need to work 'legitimately' with others so as to be of administration, we as of now help out others than most will ever know. We transmute negative vitality without acknowledging it. What's more, by taking on and transmuting these energies we are being of enormous assistance.

Additionally, Empaths are incredible audience members! Basically tuning in to another is recuperating for the one being tuned in to (except for vitality vampires) and is being of administration.

Individuals seldom tune in to others appropriately. Most are too bustling contemplating their own story, or what they need to state straightaway. Empaths do tune in and they hear on a wide range of levels. We additionally care.

There are numerous different ways Empaths help without acknowledging it, so don't stress a lot over how you ought to serve others, you as of now are.

The most ideal approach to discover your motivation is by serving yourself (support psyche, body and soul), be consistent with yourself and basically pursue your actual interests and interests... the rest will pursue.

If you do what you love and love what you do you will be upbeat... Happiness is the way to progress!

Being an empath isn't something you do, it's something you are. You have been hard-wired since birth to be like this for an explanation: to grapple the light of your spirit onto planet Earth.

The first occasion when I comprehended this idea I was truly taken by the way that most empaths I have been tutoring do have an uncommon fondness for light and anything that is of the light. The issue is that they don't understand the amount of a difference that can make on the planet if they just would let their internal light sparkle.

Empaths are here manifested during this time span on earth in consistently expanding numbers. The purpose behind being an empath during this season of change is that empaths resemble inestimable cleaners. If they decide to utilize their profound gift in administration of themselves as well as other people, their quality on this planet is the thing that makes the most significant level of change for mankind.

As a general rule the main thing that empaths are approached to do is to take a shot at themselves, which for them is exceptionally difficult to do because they are normal suppliers. Their significant life reason for existing is truly to figure out how to deal with themselves and their gift. In doing as such, they have the ability to change their lives and the lives of others in an extremely significant manner. Peruse this book on vitality clearing.

Am I An Empath? How Do I Know?

There are numerous degrees of being an empath, you can take the Empath Test here. Additionally, empaths arrive at different stages for the duration of their life. To find out additional, read this book.

If you are an empath, your spirit decided to come here on this planet and work on this part of your spirit because here an empath truly stands out!

As an empath you most likely have just felt the negative parts of this gift, as:

1. You assimilate pessimistic energies from the earth you are in, either from books, hardware or individuals. You may likewise be touchy to phantoms, discarnate substances and low energies.

2. You convey a substantial burden and it isn't yours. You are influenced by negative conduct of others and often decided to take part in negative conduct yourself so as to fit in.

3. You generally appear to realize what individuals are thinking and believing and are influenced because you care so a lot and need to help. This makes you be in mutually dependent relationships with narcissists and narrow minded individuals, who don't generally think about you.

4. You have a hard time standing up for yourself and feel exploited by relatives, companions and even outsiders.

5. By one way or another you feel liable for what befalls others in your life and wind up taking an interest in their distress. You additionally feel angry of not being valued.

How Do I Survive Being So Sensitive?

In an egotistical reality where just the childish succeed, there is no space for the individuals who have an open heart. You have presumably as of now taken in this exercise in life. However, I am here to reveal to you that this learning is just a single piece of the condition.

Since you have encountered the negative viewpoint, it's an ideal opportunity to restore the intensity of the light inside you. It's a great opportunity to realign to this undeniable gift and show to the world that strengthening and qualities originate from loving, mindful and providing for other people.

Empaths are here to instruct mankind that there is power in being a provider and that the genuine achievement is that of the spirit not of the sense of self.

Advantages of Developing Your Empathic Abilities

Individuals often reveal to me that being an empath has demolished their life. They feel bizarre, different and disengaged by the remainder of humankind. I state to them, that the spirit didn't commit an error in birthing them here.

There is a reason and the principle one is to love and grasp who you are without judgment.

In numerous spots on the web and disconnected, individuals who characterize themselves as empaths will in general jabber about how this has influenced in a negative manner. They accuse individuals in their lives and depict themselves has being mutually dependent with narcissistic characters and having battled for quite a long time to escape misuse and low self-esteem. Kindly, don't do this to yourself.

I realize that the inner self personality needs to make a feeling of show around what your identity is, however this is truly not helping your most noteworthy reason by any stretch of the imagination.

I urge you not to go into fault and victimhood mode. I do see obviously what being an empath is because I am one. Each day of my life I manage this part of myself. I used to consider it to be a revile and I felt disliked, exploited and vivaciously utilized as a dump of others cynicism and issues.

In all actuality: I likewise permitted it. At some level, the empath has an advantage in being their loved ones negative vitality vault. Because this is the way an empath feels love and appreciation. Is this proper? Obviously not! Is it part of your life way as an empath? Indeed, it is.

Glance back at your life, OK be here right currently perusing this book, if you had not experienced what you have experienced in life? Most likely not!

This is your spirit's way working through you. I am here to show you how to adore that and how to utilize your gift to enable yourself as well as other people.

When you find the intensity of this gift you will concur with me.

Being an empath is the most elevated level of otherworldly advancement accessible on this plane of the real world. If you are an empath, you are here to play this game. You have everything necessary to be effective.

Profound Benefits Of Being An Empath

These is a basic rundown of the otherworldly advantages of being an empath:

1. Your natural capacities can soar for all intents and purposes medium-term, when you figure out how to deal with your vitality. You are extremely natural, clairaudient, perceptive, clairsentient, and clairknowing. You can figure out how to take advantage of the all inclusive awareness to pick up astuteness and guidance.

2. You are an incredible manifestor! Your manifesting capacities are solid once you figure out how to utilize the intensity of aim with enthusiastic vibrational arrangement.

3. You are a characteristic healer. Your recuperating capacities will improve additional time, when you figure out how to give up and trust your vitality stream, without dreading getting depleted by others. In actuality, when you mend others, you recuperate yourself.

4. You can associate effectively with your internal direction for help and backing. Most empaths have sentiments of holy messengers helping them.

I needed to compose this book to give you that being an empath isn't a revile yet a gift. Since you are understanding your gift, you can make something happen in your life. The spirit often decides to live the negative extremity of its life exercise before it can truly get familiar with the positive one.

I accept this is valid for most empaths. Out of the blue, we start our life way in debilitation just to discover the quality and the force inside us to become what our identity is intended to be.

If you are currently encountering the negative part of being an empath, you also can make something happen if you decided to do as such. I can genuinely disclose to you that it will be hard before all else, yet certainly worth any exertion you put into it.

HOW TO SUPPORT A YOUNG EMPATH

As youngsters, we are for the most part normally empathic. As kids, we are on the whole exceptionally touchy to nature and empathic to life around us.

The issue for all of us is that, as we grow up, a dangerous and savage "framework" severely thrashes us and we become (tragically and pointlessly) separated, desensitized, and shut down subsequently. A few people, be that as it may, can't be closed down.

A few people result in these present circumstances planet officially as empaths and these individuals don't lose their association regardless of how much lethal brutality and misuse they experience. Staying empathic "regardless" might appear as though something worth being thankful for to an individual made up for lost time in the shines of Micky Mouse otherworldliness, however it ain't all wine and roses. Actually our reality is amazingly savage and dangerous: individuals who stay empathic in this world must adapt to consistent defenselessness and steady introduction to a rough, poisonous stew heaved at them by family, companions, work partners, and (progressively) complete outsiders.

I got the chance to let you know, it is difficult for them. It harms them, harms them, and in the long haul, it wrecks a large number of them. The primary concern is, poisonous quality gathers throughout the decades and in the end, the physical unit separates. Indeed, even the most grounded empath in the end clasps if not appropriately secured and bolstered.

The inquiry before us today is, how would you appropriately secure and bolster an empath? It is a basic inquiry. In this short book, I would prefer not to manage the assail and over-burden grown-up empath. That is a major point that requires expanded treatment. Rather, in this book, I need to give a touch of direction to guardians and educators on the most proficient method to prepare and secure their empathic kids. Before I get into that, be that as it may, I simply need to state that the counsel I'll be offering here is very different than the guidance empaths (and those related with them) typically get. Normally, empaths (and those related with them) are given what I would call "exclusively engaged" exhortation. Separately engaged guidance is exhortation coordinated only at the empath.

When empaths (and the individuals related with them) get this kind of counsel, they are advised basically that it is up to the empath to adapt!

Empaths are informed that if they need to have the option to "bargain" with their gifts, they will need to figure out how to "adapt" with the real world. So as to adapt, they should "reframe" their standpoint, clean their home, cry and express, use gems to purify vitality, construct a few limits, perceive their celestial crucial, so on (see this book for a prime model). I'm certain if you've at any point run over the "standard" exhortation given to empaths, you'll be acquainted with the direction given.

Sadly, I need to state, independently engaged adapting systems truly don't help the empath because the issue isn't the empath, the issue is the dangerous condition they should persevere. Independently engaged adapting methodologies are exceptionally dangerous because they either overlook the significance of the conditions' effect on the empath or acknowledge nature in which the empath moves as an unchangeable, even profoundly attractive given.

These methodologies take the savagery and poisonous quality of this planet with a "well, that is simply life, better become acclimated to it" disposition. A few defenders of independently engaged procedures even venture to state that all the harmfulness and viciousness that empaths experience is some sort of profound "test" or "exercise." They state to the enduring empath, "what doesn't execute you makes you more grounded" and they leave it precisely at that.

Yet, that is in this way, so off-base.

Empaths are here as healers to help the individuals of this planet recuperate and push ahead. Empaths are particularly delicate and in order "emissaries of Consciousness/Spirit" and it isn't their business to adapt and acknowledge. Despite what might be expected, we must shield them from savagery and misuse so we can ensure that they remain sound and entire with the goal that they can grow up and carry out the responsibility they came here to do.

Do ya got that?

If an empath falls under the harmful weight of this planet, it is our disappointment, not theirs.

Presently, if you don't mind comprehend, it doesn't all tumble to you. Conditions helpful for sound empathy require essential worldwide change and that is something we are for the most part must partake in. Obviously, that doesn't imply that we need to trust that worldwide change will begin fixing things. There are things that you can do beginning right currently to improve conditions for the profoundly delicate empaths in your lives and one of the most significant, significant, and open things we would all be able to do is to secure every one of the offspring of this world.

As noted over, all people are empathic in adolescence and some empathics are especially open and associated. If we need our youngsters to grow up empathic and if we need our empaths to grow up sound, entire, enabled, and prepared to mend, we need to begin by ensuring them during the most defenseless long periods of their lives - in youth and pre-adulthood.

I am certain you will concur. It is the long stretches of our youth and youthfulness when we are generally helpless against grown-up attack and it is in the long stretches of youth and immaturity that we are most needing security. In view of that, here are a few things that guardians, instructors, scout pioneers, and other people who are day by day engaged with kids can do to begin making living conditions that are sound, steady, defensive, and helpful for the improvement of completely working empathic healers; (also completely working and empathic individuals).

Guardians AND TEACHERS

Perceive that empaths exist: The main thing guardians and instructors can would if they like to help and secure empaths is to just understand that empaths exist. This is a significant initial step. If you don't accept that empaths really exist, then you won't put any psychological vitality into seeing them, substantially less make conditions that help and bolster them. We as a whole need to figure out how to see empaths in our condition; else, we'll get not even close to near making a difference. In this way, the initial step is to just accept that empaths exist and in this manner put some psychological exertion into seeing them in your general surroundings.

Comprehend empaths: Once guardians and educators have perceived that empaths exist, the subsequent stage is to endeavor to get them and fortunately, that isn't advanced science.

To comprehend empaths, just see how they act and interface with others and how others act and connect with them. For our motivations here, the absolute most significant thing to watch and comprehend about empaths is that they are profoundly touchy to physical and non-physical, immediate and backhanded, dynamic and uninvolved ambush.

Ambushes of various types hurt an empath. Shouting, hollering, boisterous attack, verbally abusing, detached forceful jokes, avoidance, self-important negligence, putting down punches, and even just arbitrarily diffused, non-coordinated energies of outrage, antagonistic vibe, sorrow, and despondency can hurt the empath! As noted, numerous individuals desensitize themselves so they are never again mindful of the agony, however empaths can't desensitize thus they are continually helpless and presented to ambush. This is a significant thing that you ought to consistently remember. Regardless of how solid you figure somebody may be, ambush them enough, trouble them with enough poisonous mental and enthusiastic muck, and they inevitably breakdown under the strain.

Perceive Reality: Speaking about dangerous muck, the third thing guardians and instructors can do to support the empathic youngster (or grown-up) is to perceive the genuine idea of our existence on this planet. This is significant. The picture that Hollywood presents to us, the picture that such a significant number of us accept and take a stab at, is bogus. We don't live in an I-Carly, Happy Days, Leave it to Beaver sort of world. Our families are broken, our general public is rough, and our social communications are noticeably shallow and frequently poisonous.

Actually, kids on this planet are misled, beaten, mishandled, misused, and assaulted each second of consistently. Indeed, even apparently blameless "sleepovers" or "scout excursions" can open our youngsters to danger, misuse, and rape and this isn't to make reference to kid abuse, kid work, kid erotic entertainment, etc.

This planet is a poisonous soup for youngsters and that is the truth. Denying it, imagining it isn't there, discovering profound advantage in savagery and misuse, or basically overlooking it (out of the blue) won't keep the kids from being mishandled and empaths from being wrecked. If you need to help the empath, open your eyes and see.

Perceive that harm occurs: One you see and comprehend the empath and once you are in line with the real world and not dream, the following thing is to understand that if you open empaths to reality as it right now seems to be, harm happens. If you hit an empath, if you shout at them, if you control them, if you abuse their vitality, if you ambush them, if you disparage them, if you assault them, if you attempt to confound them, if you absorb them the irregular energies of diffuse anguish and gloom, harm gathers similarly that harm would accumulate if you cut them with a knife.

You can imagine that isn't the situation or perhaps mitigate your complicity and blame by making statements like "what doesn't murder you makes you more grounded" or "it's their decision to be here" or some other profound/Darwinian garbage like that, however if you do, you're self-bamboozled. Ambush a youngster, assault and empath beat another individual for reasons unknown, and you're harming them and causing them harm, period.

Comprehend that harm sets aside a long effort to mend: Once you comprehend the genuine idea of the empath and the peril they are in, then comprehend that enthusiastic, mental, and otherworldly harm that empaths cause because of Toxic Socialization can take a very long time to recuperate. Physical harm can take as meager as a couple of days to mend, however as researchers and others are starting to acknowledge, passionate/mental/soul.

Issue a NO ABUSE announcement: One you perceive the genuine idea of this world, when you perceive that empaths are in steady peril, when you perceive the high, long haul cost and the genuine need to secure our kids, the following thing that you should do is STOP THE VIOLENCE any place you can. Issue a "NO ABUSE" announcement. In our home, we have zero resilience for maltreatment of any sort. In our home, no one is permitted to shout, call names, regurgitate pessimism, take part in dynamic or uninvolved ambush; or something else, be adverse toward someone else.

This doesn't imply that we are not basic or open, yet it means that we attempt to impart in a positive way consistently. We're not great and passionate attacks do occur (and its quite often the grown-ups who are the culprits and the kids who are the people in question), however when they do, the culprit is relied upon to be responsible and issue an earnest statement of regret. Contrasted with the youth that we had and contrasted with the adolescence of numerous children even today, our house is a strict Eden, as it ought to be.

We need our kids to grow up sound, entire, associated, and empathic and this won't occur if we endure any type of attack. What's more, note, the equivalent "no maltreatment" rule ought to be received by educators in schools also. Instructors disgracing kids, youngsters disgracing one another, and any type of mental, enthusiastic, or profound brutality ought not go on without serious consequences in the class or on the schoolyard in any way, shape or form. Attack of any sort harms the empath doubly so. Perceive that there is no spot or space for maltreatment in the life of the youngster and issue a "no maltreatment" declaration.

Ensure your kids/secure the kids: Issuing a "no maltreatment" decree is just the main solid advance forward that you can take.

When you have declared your decision and want to live in a maltreatment free condition, push for its help, appropriation, and requirement. Furthermore, recall, the house isn't the main spot that kids and empaths endure ambush. Misuse occurs at school, at grandmothers, at aunts, at work, among "companions, etc. You can't control where a grown-up goes, yet you can shield kids from presentation to mishandle, so there is no reason. Never open empathic youngsters to manhandle.

Keep youngsters far, far away from lethal grown-ups and their dangerous little kids, particularly as kids develop. Play dates in the initial not many years are generally innocuous, in any event, when guardians are exceptionally poisonous. In any case, danger inevitably seeps into youngsters who can start to carry on in lethal manners toward other kids; so in the end, much other kids (particularly other kids!) become the culprits of viciousness.

Every single other thing creatures equivalent, as empathic kids develop, they become increasingly presented and helpless to cynicism. The initial barely any years that youngsters play together is no difficulty, however by ten, twelve, and past, harmfulness and misuse experienced in families begins to overflow. Therefore, ensure your kids, youths, and youthful grown-ups from other youngsters, teenagers, and grown-ups as they develop. You may imagine that pushing your kids into family and social circumstances is a positive thing, yet it is often not. When it comes to securing the up and coming age of empaths, adopt a no-bargain strategy; ensure your eyes are all the way open.

Train your youngsters well: without a doubt guardians and educators must secure kids because they don't have the ability to ensure themselves. Be that as it may, youngsters grow up to be grown-ups and guardians and instructors should in the long run release control. When youngsters become grown-ups, it is dependent upon them to ensure themselves; be that as it may, they can possibly do this if they have been instructed what to do.

They don't realize what to do by enchantment! Guardians and instructors need to show youngsters how to secure themselves, how to adapt to antagonism, how to fabricate limits, how to dismiss misuse, and how to maintain a strategic distance from harmfulness. I've composed books focused on youngsters, to help pass on fundamental data.

Also, fundamental otherworldly counsel is given in my Great Awakening: Concepts and Techniques for Successful Spiritual Practice, yet there are interesting points right away. One of the most significant things that you can instruct your kid is that there will never be any reason for misuse. If you instruct them that there is no reason for misuse, then they will grow up maintaining a strategic distance from it, dismissing it, and declining to acknowledge it.

If you instruct them that misuse is OK at times (like for instance, as "discipline"), then they will now and then think that its difficult to remove themselves from damaging circumstances. Keep in mind, harm accumulates when empaths, kids, and even grown-ups experience misuse. Instruct empaths/kids/grown-ups that there will never be any justification for misuse, so that if misuse fires up, they realize they should leave. This is particularly significant for empaths. Misuse harms everyone; kids and empaths doubly so. Therefore, empaths must be educated from the very beginning that no measure of physical, enthusiastic, sexual, mental, or otherworldly maltreatment is adequate.

Presently, training youngsters to dismiss all types of misuse may sound basic and direct; however actually, numerous individuals will battle forcefully with this. Think about this: the essential message that guardians and instructors send to kids is that it is OK to hurt another human if they merit it. The message that youngsters get is "if someone accomplishes something terrible, feel free to hurt them".

We may not obviously talk this message to our kids, yet it is demonstrated to them practically every day by guardians, educators, and grown-up power figures who appear to experience no difficulty shouting, hollering, hitting, harming, disgracing, deprecating, and generally ambushing the exposed youngster whenever the kid accomplishes something "incorrectly".

We attack our children and afterward to justify it, we reveal to them that they merit it. What's more, that is only the beginning. As youngsters grow up, they hear the message and see it displayed over and over and once more. When we are completely developed, we can justify significant degrees of misuse, even torment, by essentially disclosing to ourselves that the individuals we are harming "merit" to be harmed because they accomplished something terrible. The message is perfectly clear. Our children learn - we as a whole discover that as long as someone "merits it", we can hurt them with relative exemption.

Yet, that thought and that message isn't right, off-base, wrong. That message needs to change and it needs to change at the present time. We as a people, as a country, and as a planet, need to get it through our obstinate empty heads that there is no reason for misuse. Regardless of what the youngster, juvenile, or grown-up does, misuse is never an alternative.

Discipline is ambush - unadulterated and basic. Individuals are once in a while "amended" or "transformed" by misuse. Normally, they are simply harmed considerably more.

There is no advantage. Attack harms like damnation and it causes weakening long haul harm to the body/mind. This is particularly so when we think about our empathic kids (and recollect, all kids are normally empathic). If we need them to grow up sound, entire, and solid, we need to quit hitting, harming, hollering, and beating.

You can help with that by halting the maltreatment, yet additionally, by sending an unmistakable, often rehashed verbal message to the kids and teenagers of this world that misuse isn't OK. Try not to show the kids to endure it, show the youngsters to identify it, maintain a strategic distance from it when they see it, report it to individuals who can secure them, and oppose it whenever they can (for example when it doesn't further imperil them).

Invest bunches of value energy: Even however the world ought to be significantly superior to anything it is presently, the world will never be an ideal spot. In any case, even in a perfect world, there will at present be times when attack will happen. We're all in a human body all things considered and the human body at times gains out of power.

Yet, that is OK because people, empaths included, are versatile. Despite the fact that in this book, I stress that empaths are amazingly touchy, they are not frail little masses of yellow passionate jam. When they are not set upon by years/many years of misuse, when they have been instructed to fabricate safe spaces and limits, when they have been educated to dismiss misuse - at the end of the day, when they are not methodicallly stifled and harmed, they are solid and flexible. We can manage the aftermath of someone's loss of control because the physical body is flexible. It has worked in adapting and mending components and these systems, if they are working and appropriately "charged", can manage even profound injury. You can guarantee these components are working and appropriately charged by just giving out parcels and loads of affection.

At home, this implies heaps of embraces, love, consideration, and backing. At school, this implies loads of positive respect, consideration, and backing. It ought to abandon saying, yet empathic youngsters - all kids truth be told, need bunches of consideration, heaps of affection, loads of proper physical contact, and parcels and parts and bunches of help: unquestionably more than they at present get. As a parent, we will knock facing time constraints in our day.

Educators will knock facing class sizes and regulatory right. My recommendation to guardians is to organize your children's' enthusiastic and mental needs over beverages with the young men, mother's espresso club, etc. My recommendation to educators - train yourself to focus and push your colleagues (and governments) to quit spending on death (for example war) and start going through on time on earth. We are rich social orders and, with a shift in need away from an affluent age and toward profoundly adjusted, human-focused economies, we can without much of a stretch manage the cost of a lot littler class sizes.

Innovatively, financially, we have all that we have to make ideal world. Launch governments that are "by the rich, for the rich". Choose governments by the individuals and for the individuals. As guardians and instructors, we are the ones that must demonstration to choose governments that will organize our youngsters and teenagers.

Haul them out of school: Finally, if you happen to have the fortitude and the help, haul your children out of school. Schools are presently one of the most dangerous situations on earth (and if you don't trust me, focus whenever a youthful immature ends it all or goes shooting to bring others down too). Schools are second just to the home as the essential site of viciousness and misuse.

My book here on psychological mistreatment in schools and the all-inclusive critique it has gotten uncovers how terrible it tends to be. If you can and if there are bolsters in your general vicinity for self-teaching, haul your youngsters out of school and instruct them at home. Obviously, do this just if you have the methods and just if you can give them quality training at home.

We need our youngsters to be instructed and it is getting progressively workable for a few, at any rate. In the Canadian territory where I live, our administration is creating on the web educational plans that understudies can plug into from any place they happen to be! Our family is lucky to have a formal self-teach choice, for example, this. Our children take genuine school classes, communicate with genuine understudies and instructors, study a similar educational plan, and accomplish similar outcomes while concentrating from the wellbeing of our home. It has had an enormous and constructive outcome in their intelligent person, enthusiastic, and mental improvement; in this way, if you can do it, do it. If not, push for it. Governments can do a great deal to make conditions that are strong of self-teaching. Until schools tidy up and start attempting to make a protected situation for our empathic kids (for all youngsters), push governments to give choices.

Change the world: My last guidance to guardians, instructors, and truly anyone listening is to change the world. At last, this is the best way to totally secure our empathic youngsters and grown-ups and we unquestionably need to do that. We have all endured grievous degrees of affliction and maltreatment for far, unreasonably long.

We have viewed our guiltless kids grow up hurt, harmed, discouraged, and even self-destructive. In the dreams of our media and the wars of our rulers, we see the result of savagery and misuse. If we need things to transform, we need to quit accusing the people in question, we need to quit encouraging our empaths to "adapt", and we need to begin changing the world so their full mending/empathic potential can be at long last figured it out. Keep in mind, empaths are here to assist us with mending and change. They can possibly do that if we quit attacking them, quit harming them, and start sustaining, securing, and appropriately supporting them and the work they came to do.

HOW TO BECOME AN ASSERTIVE EMPATH

This is the battle of an empath: to feel and to mind so profoundly that the idea of causing someone else torment or distress actually turns into your own torment and distress. To abstain from frustrating somebody, you consent to help despite the fact that now you'll need to reshuffle your effectively stuffed calendar. You would prefer not to be unfriendly, so you welcome the startling visitor in despite the fact that it's an awful time. You would prefer not to be uncompassionate, so you tune in to your companion's tragic account for the 14,000th time.

Also, what happens then?

Indeed, because we're empaths, it begins to influence our vitality. Empaths resemble strolling batteries of vitality. Others, often those needing a "vitality fix", are attracted to empaths like moths to a fire. Without significance to, they will rapidly deplete your vitality, leaving you depleted and angry.

Individuals with profoundly empathic characters will in general battle most with being self-assured. Be that as it may, it is empaths who often need emphaticness aptitudes the most. While defining and holding limits can make us break an apprehensive perspiration, they are critical and vital. Without limits, we will drain vitality quicker than we can produce it. We have none left over for any other person, or in any event, for ourselves.

It would be ideal if you note: I am a member in offshoot programs, including Amazon.com. This page may incorporate subsidiary connections that will take you to an outer site. Any buy you make in the wake of tapping on one of these connections will acquire me a little commission at not a penny of additional expense to you. Concerned? Need to know more? No issues. Head to my Privacy Policy and Affiliate Disclosure for more data.

Moreover, inability to define up limits, especially with the individuals who sequentially break them, causes disdain. It influences your vitality around that individual. Hatred is a guileful toxin. It destroys your relationship until you may do hopeless harm which could have been kept away from with sound limits.

Why empaths battle with being decisive

Often our dread of going to bat for ourselves and stating our limits originates from a dread that if we are emphatic or defined a limit it will adversely affect the relationship.

In our general public, since the beginning, we are instructed to relate prize and discipline dependent on how well we can satisfy others' desires. If we satisfied our folks or instructors, we were a "decent young lady". If, in any case, we conflicted with their desires, we were acting mischievously and often rebuffed. At the end of the day, we were educated to satisfy the outside world (guardians/educators and so forth) and disregard our impulses and inward direction.

Expressions, for example,

"Try not to argue"

"Because I said as much"

"Give that toy to your sibling – you need to share"

"Try not to be narrow minded"

"Choose not to retaliate"

"No, please, you need to give Aunty Agnes a nestle"

"Be pleasant"

... which were all spoken with the best goals by guardians and individuals in positions in power, intuitively instructed us:

That there were others on the planet who were better than us

That our own needs/needs/sentiments were invalid

To put others' needs and needs before our own, even at the sacrifice of our own

Not to defend ourselves in strife

That our own feeling of limits and solace levels were less significant than planning something for please others.

So, a considerable lot of us were unknowingly instructed that our very own limits, needs, and needs were less significant than those of others. We regularly made expressions like those imply that it was not alright to go to bat for and attest our own privileges or set sound limits with others. We discovered that it was progressively critical to get things done to satisfy others.

As we develop into adulthood, it turns out to be progressively difficult to "unlearn" individuals satisfying conduct – even as we're stating "yes" while our inward being is shouting, "Gracious God, please NO!"

Signs you have feeble limits or battle with emphaticness

You have difficult or sensational relationships with individuals in your life, often based on them exceeding or making you feel awkward.

You're somewhat of a fiasco at deciding.

You put everybody's needs before your own.

You consequently concede to individuals you see to have a degree of power over you.

You're on edge that if you draw a limit or state no it may cost you your relationship.

You feel as though individuals misconstrue you a great deal or don't regard you.

Your conduct has begun to drift into the aloof forceful.

You will in general restrain your emotions and afterward haphazardly detonate.

For what reason being confident is significant

The most significant thing to comprehend about your limits is that you reserve a privilege to them. Limits are not something just narrow minded individuals have. (Truth be told, if you are stressed over being "narrow minded", you're presumably not. The most narrow minded individuals often never stress over being egotistical.)

Your limits are NOT there to rebuff others. Truth be told, your limits are not about any other person by any stretch of the imagination. Your limits are to secure you – your vitality, wellbeing, enthusiastic wellbeing and your relationships.

Being decisive won't harm your relationships with others (in any event, not the individuals who are really put resources into you). Indeed, being self-assured will really help ensure your relationships.

It appears to be irrational, yet neglecting to be confident and build up clear limits can harm your relationships. Without a doubt, in saying no or being confident there may be some transient frustration, distress and even indignation from the other individual (especially if they are not used to you defining limits). Eventually however, when you don't talk your fact, and rather stifle how you truly feel, you will become angry.

Without you knowing it, this hatred that you develop makes you subliminally produce a negative vitality. The other individual will get on it, intentionally or unknowingly. What's more, as the law of fascination lets us know, what you oppose endures. That pessimistic vitality will just draw in business as usual from the other individual.

Notwithstanding, straightforwardly saying no or defining a limit attracts your line the sand. It enables the other individual to unmistakably know where you stand. It gives them a system for how to interface with you viably, without the mystery. This implies less errors and therefore, less clash over the long haul.

There are numerous advantages to being confident:

You will be a superior communicator: It doesn't make a difference whether you're managing your significant other, your mom, your chief, or new individuals. Being self-assured enables you to convey what needs be all the more unquestionably. You will have the option to express what is on your mind concisely and tranquilly. You're less inclined to run into mistaken assumptions.

You will have more prominent confidence: When we respect our very own needs we let ourselves know "you are deserving of regard". This upgrades our mental self-portrait as well as improves the degree of regard we draw from others.

You can step all the more completely into your authentic self: You never need to stow away any longer or claim to be somebody else. What you bring to your relationships will be progressively authentic, veritable and alluring. You will be harmonious in feeling, thought, word and activity. Consider the amount all the more clear and attractive your vitality will be!

It makes you increasingly affable: People are attracted to others when they know where they remain with them. When you can obviously convey your needs and needs to other people, you show individuals how to treat you. You give them that you are fit for settling on your own choices and have restrains on the conduct you are eager to endure.

When individuals see you have an unmistakable course and a sound confidence, they are bound to regard you and less inclined to attempt to coax you around to their perspective or convince you to accomplish something you're not happy with. Your eagerness to be certified, straightforward and forthright urges others to do likewise, and individuals love others who permit them that opportunity. They will cherish that when they address you, they know where they stand and they additionally feel regarded and heard. They will cherish that they are set up for accomplishment in their cooperations with you by realizing how best to convey.

Less nervousness and misery: We can really lessen social tension and cumbersomeness by going up against our dread of being decisive or confronting showdown. After a couple of nerve-wracking first endeavors, we before long discover that it isn't as unnerving as we once first idea.

When we request what we need and build up limits, we make more space in our lives for what we do need, prompting an all the more satisfying and easeful experience of life, which thusly raises our state of mind. You will feel more in charge of your life, which is fabulous manifestation magic!

It's normal for exceptionally delicate individuals (HSPs) to battle with being decisive, as in, going to bat for one's privileges and qualities in a valuable and quiet manner. Because of their tranquil manner, individuals may talk over them and dismissal their emotions and perspectives. Because HSPs can be effectively harmed, they hate forceful correspondence, and many would keep away from struggle all together, trusting that the issue would just run its course.

As a HSP, I find that I battle with struggle. In my first year at college, I didn't coexist with my flat mates. One flat mate often scrutinized me for not sufficiently cleaning her dishes as we pivoted doing this task.

Her contention appeared to be unfair thinking about that she had not done a lot of housekeeping, yet I was reluctant to go up against her. Rather, I held an unfortunate resentment towards her during the whole time that we were flat mates.

I presently understand that in spite of the fact that HSPs battle with struggle and are every now and again being stepped on by others, it doesn't imply that they can't be self-assured. I accept that it's a matter of figuring out how to control our feelings, set limits, and convey our musings better.

The following are 5 hints to help HSPs become increasingly emphatic:

1. Set limits.

Because HSPs are insightful of others' sentiments and often have elevated levels of empathy, they may end up turning into a passionate dumping ground for others.

As a HSP and an empath, I end up entering unfortunate relationships with expectations of sparing the other individual, where I then become harmed because the relationship is too uneven. I understand that it's essential to take control in these circumstances by defining limits.

Are your feelings preventing you from pushing ahead? I can show you how to carry on with an increasingly engaged, satisfying life—in a sheltered, nonjudgmental condition. Gain more from our accomplice Brenda Knowles.

Often times, I can turn out to be extremely consumed by someone else's reality and neglect to deal with myself first. What has helped me figure out how to adhere to a meaningful boundary is understanding that there is just so a lot of I can accomplish for other people, and that I can't deal with others if I don't deal with myself first. The vast majority would comprehend when you let them realize that you need time to revive and that it's nothing close to home on their end.

2. Convey your emotions through decisive composition.

When it comes to managing struggle, I discover it profoundly helpful to impart the issue(s) in composed words. In addition to the fact that this provides quick cleansing discharge, yet it likewise carries lucidity to the circumstance and is a powerful apparatus for open correspondence. Something critical to remember when composing a letter about your contention with somebody is to utilize "I feel" explanations. These announcements are significant because they state the circumstance so it mirrors your viewpoint and enthusiastic needs without putting direct fault on the other individual.

A self-assured letter ought to clarify the circumstance as compactly as would be prudent, without diving into superfluous subtleties. Here's a format for you to attempt:

Dear _____,

In spite of the fact that it's difficult for me to raise this subject, I feel that it's important to examine this (contention/misconception). Because I have a feeling that I can more readily convey what needs be recorded as a hard copy, I've decided to keep in touch with you a letter.

Recently, I've been feeling harmed about (embed circumstance). When (the circumstance) occurs, I feel as if I (what enthusiastic need isn't met).

This has been burdening me and I would prefer not to leave it uncertain. I would acknowledge if we can fix this soon, yet regardless of whether we can't, I simply needed you to realize how I'm feeling.

Truly,

You

3. Be aware of how you present yourself.

An individual's pledge decision and non-verbal communication can uncover a great deal about them. HSPs might be unreasonably unassuming to their benefit, and shockingly, others may see this as an indication of shortcoming and attempt to exploit them. There are sure expressions and words that ought to be maintained a strategic distance from so as to sound progressively decisive:

Simply—this word limits the intensity of an announcement and causes you to appear to be guarded and regretful.

I'm no master, however... — this discourse propensity manifests to abstain from sounding pushy or haughty, yet doing so nullifies the validity of the announcement.

I can't—this is an aloof proclamation and infers losing power over your activities.

Consider the possibility that we attempted... ?— expressing a thought as an inquiry welcomes rejoinders and is paid attention to not exactly direct explanations.

Sorry–saying 'sorry' for things pointlessly puts on a show of being contemptible, however it additionally makes you less confident.

Much obliged! :)— abusing outcry imprints and emoticons may suggest that you're unreliable and worried about being seen as kind, commendable, and affable.

When it comes to non-verbal communication, some body motions, for example, crossed arms, shoulder slouching, and absence of eye to eye connection could show protectiveness and an absence of certainty. An extraordinary method to improve your non-verbal communication is through open talking. Join an open talking club or work on talking before a camera to fabricate certainty and stage nearness.

4. Try not to think about things literally.

For HSPs, this is more difficult than one might expect. Yet, remember that individuals often venture their negative feelings onto others because they battle to adapt to their very own issues. Recognizing this has helped me make a channel and think about things less literally.

I additionally attempt to comprehend why I feel guarded in specific circumstances and perceive that thinking about things also literally gives certain people more control over me than they merit. As Eleanor Rooselvelt says, "Nobody can make you feel substandard without your assent."

5. Assume responsibility for your joy.

At long last, I've discovered that my bliss doesn't rely upon others. Thinking about what others consider me, requiring individuals' approval, and not giving myself an opportunity to unwind and inhale makes me hopeless. The following are a few statements that I find moving when it comes to assuming responsibility for my very own joy:

"Life's too short to even consider caring what others think." — obscure

"In any case, what is satisfaction with the exception of the basic amicability between a man and the life he leads?" — Albert Camus

"The joy of your life relies on the nature of your considerations: therefore, watch in like manner, and take care that you engage no ideas unsatisfactory to excellence and sensible nature.

HOW TO BECOME AN EXTROVERTED EMPATH

Most by far of empaths would, when asked, presumably name themselves as thoughtful person or with withdrawn propensities.

There are, be that as it may, a significant minority of empaths and exceptionally delicate people who are especially outgoing individuals.

You might not have contemplated yourself in these terms previously, however if you can identify with a large portion of the accompanying focuses, there is a decent possibility you are an outgoing empath.

1. You Feel Alive Around Others, But Mostly In Small Groups

As a social butterfly, you completely appreciate investing energy with others and you can without much of a stretch while away the hours in the organization of companions.

It doesn't make a difference whether you are wandering into the wilds of nature, getting some food, or playing some game, you simply love to be among others.

You do, be that as it may, like to keep the gathering size genuinely little when meeting up with individuals because you discover it such a great amount of simpler to adapt to.

Your extroversion and your capacities as an empath both mean you absorb the vitality of everyone around you and it's critical to you to keep these fair.

An excessive number of particular energies and it's somewhat similar to adding an ever increasing number of fixings to a mixed drink – inevitably it winds up as an unpalatable wreckage.

2. You Are Very Choosy About Who You Spend Time With

As much as you appreciate being in the organization of others, you won't simply make due with any old individual.

All things considered, you are an empath and this makes you extremely delicate to the vibrations radiated by others.

If you have a decision between being in the organization of somebody with negative vitality and being distant from everyone else, you'd take the singular street without fail.

You are glad to meet new individuals, however if it before long turns out to be certain that they are emitting a vibe that doesn't orchestrate with your own, you discover a reason to leave.

3. You Are Very Choosy About What You Spend Time Doing

While your standard social butterfly may be glad to oblige others in whatever action has been recommended, the empath within you thinks that its difficult to get enthused by things you have no enthusiasm for.

It feels inauthentic to participate in something that you'd lean toward not to do, thus you are glad to turn down a greeting if it doesn't put a smile on your face.

This doesn't mean you are requesting and resolute – you simply know when and when not to say yes.

4. You Experience Swings Of Energy

An outgoing empath needs to adapt to an exceptionally fascinating difficulty which can prompt unexpected and extraordinary swings in vitality levels.

As an outgoing individual, you can recharge your batteries through contact with others, yet as an empath, you additionally ingest energies from surrounding you.

While you can without much of a stretch go days or even a long time in outgoing individual mode, there will quite often come a point where your battery becomes cheated and you hamper.

Your eagerness and fervor for seeing others immediately dives as you battle to ingest any more vitality, and you pull back into yourself.

For some time, your outgoing side goes on break to permit your vitality levels to try and out again.

While you may just need to escape to your internal cavern for a brief period, it can once in a while be that you go on a psychological get-away for up to seven days.

In this time, you nearly tumble off the radar to the extent mingling goes.

5. You Like To Plan Events In Advance

As much as you appreciate getting out on the town with others, you likewise want to plan such social affairs ahead of time.

Regardless of whether it's only a day or two's notification, you like to have the option to diarize and rationally get ready for the prospective celebrations.

The purpose behind this is because you realize how simple it is for your internal empath to become overpowered.

A few circumstances will include more noteworthy quantities of companions, others will mean investigating absolutely new places, despite everything others, may mean gathering altogether new individuals.

Every one of these things are potential risks to an emapth, so you like to have admonishing so as to make a psychological shield.

IMPROVE YOUR SELF-ESTEEM

Low confidence is shockingly a self-fulling prediction. The more awful you feel about what your identity is and what you do, the less inspiration you'll need to take the necessary steps to construct your confidence.

From that point it's anything but difficult to winding down into a cycle of negative and round reasoning, keeping you buried in harming - and mistaken - convictions.

How might you stop this endless loop and start moving yourself a progressively positive way?

It's a procedure, and it won't occur incidentally, however there are things you can do to kick it off and keep it moving. Here are 20 ground-breaking approaches to improve your confidence rapidly so as to begin feeling increasingly certain.

1. Ace another ability.

When you become gifted in something that compares with your abilities and interests, you increment your feeling of competency.

2. Rundown your achievements.

Consider every one of the things you've cultivated, then record them.

Make a rundown of all that you've done that you feel glad for, all that you've progressed nicely. Survey your rundown when you need a token of your capacity to complete things and to do them well.

3. Accomplish something inventive.

Inventive errands are an incredible method to return the stream to your life. Innovativeness invigorates the mind, so the more you use it, the more noteworthy the advantages. Haul out your old guitar, compose a story or sonnet, take a move class or pursue a network theater creation. When you include the test of having a go at something new, it encourages you considerably more.

4. Get clear on your qualities.

Figure out what your qualities are and look at your life to see where you're not living in arrangement with what you accept. Then roll out any essential improvements. The more you realize a big motivator for you, the more sure you will be.

5. Challenge your restricting convictions.

When you find yourself contemplating yourself, stop and challenge yourself. Try not to leave yourself alone constrained by wrong convictions.

6. Remain at edge of your usual range of familiarity.

Stretch yourself and move to the edge of your usual range of familiarity.

Get awkward - have a go at something new, meet different individuals or approach a circumstance in a whimsical manner. Certainty starts at the edge of your usual range of familiarity.

7. Help somebody.

Utilize your gifts, aptitudes and capacities to help other people. Give somebody direct help, share supportive assets or encourage somebody something they need to learn. Offer something you do well as a gift to somebody.

8. Recuperate your past.

Uncertain issues and show can keep you caught in low confidence. Look for the help of a prepared advisor to assist you with mending the past so you can move onto the future in a certain and confident manner.

9. Quit agonizing over what others think.

When you stress over what others will consider you, you never don't hesitate to be totally yourself. Settle on a firm choice to quit agonizing over what others think- - start settling on decisions dependent on what you need, not what you think others need from you.

10. Peruse something moving.

An incredible method to acquire confidence is to peruse something that lifts you up and makes you feel positive about yourself.

11. Recover your trustworthiness.

Characterize what trustworthiness implies for you, and guarantee that you're living as per that comprehension. If your life isn't lined up with your character, it will deplete you and leave you feeling terrible about yourself.

12. Release contrary individuals.

If there are individuals in your life who are negative- - who have nothing positive to state or who put you down or exploit you- - do the shrewd thing and let them go. The best way to locate your confidence is to encircle yourself with steady constructive individuals who appreciate you and worth you.

13. Attract a line the sand.

The most ideal approach to locate your confidence is to make individual limits. Recognize what your limits are and how you wish to react when individuals cross them. Try not to enable others to control you, exploit you or control you. To be certain is to keep up firm limits.

14. Care about your appearance.

When you put your best self forward, you feel your best. Dress like somebody who has certainty and let your confidence come through by they way you look.

15. Welcome disappointment as a feature of development.

It's a typical reaction to be difficult for yourself when you've fizzled. Yet, if you can shift your deduction to comprehend that disappointment is a chance to realize, that it assumes an essential job in learning and development, it can assist you with keeping viewpoint.

Recall too that disappointment implies you're attempting.

16. Continuously stay an understudy.

Consider yourself a lifelong student. Approach everything that you do with an understudy's mindset - what Zen Buddhists call Shoshin or "apprentice's brain"- - open, anxious, unprejudiced and ready to learn.

17. Face your dread.

Enable yourself to feel apprehensive yet prop up in any case. Confidence is often found in the move between your most profound wants and your biggest feelings of dread.

18. Become a tutor.

Be there for somebody who needs your direction, your initiative and your help. Their regard and appreciation - and watching them progress with your assistance - will add to your confidence and sense of pride.

19. Characterize achievement.

Clarify what achievement intends to you and what it implies as far as your certainty. If you truly need to accomplish something you should locate the confidence inside yourself to do what needs to be done.

EMPATH AND NARCISSIST

Opposites are drawn toward each other — or so we are told. While this standard can possibly expand your perspectives, individuals who are complete opposites may be drawn together for all an inappropriate reasons.

Narcissists, for instance, are pulled in to individuals they will get the best use from. Often, this implies they seek after and target empaths.

Empaths are something contrary to narcissists. While individuals with narcissistic character issue have no empathy, and flourish with the requirement for appreciation, empaths are profoundly touchy and in line with others' feelings.

Empaths are "passionate wipes," who can assimilate sentiments from others effectively. This makes them exceptionally alluring to narcissists, because they see somebody who will satisfy all their needs in a magnanimous manner.

A 'lethal' fascination bound for debacle

Judith Orloff, a specialist and creator of "The Empath's Survival Guide," revealed to Business Insider this is a harmful fascination which is bound for debacle.

"What narcissists see in empaths is a giving, loving individual who is going to attempt to be given to you and love you and hear you out," she said. "In any case, shockingly empaths are pulled in to narcissists, because from the outset this is about a bogus self. Narcissists present a bogus self, where they can appear to be beguiling and insightful, and in any event, giving, until you don't do things their way, and afterward they get cold, retaining and rebuffing."

When a narcissist is attempting to snare somebody in, they will be loving and mindful, however their cover before long begins to slip. Toward the starting they just observe the great characteristics, and accept the relationship will make them look great. This doesn't last because narcissists are loaded with hatred, and they consider most to be as underneath them. When they begin to see their accomplice's blemishes, they never again admire them, and they begin to reprimand them for not being great.

It can now and then take some time for the real nature to appear, Orloff stated, so she discloses to her customers to never become hopelessly enamored with a narcissist. Be that as it may, this conflicts with an empath's impulses, as they accept they can fix individuals and recuperate anything with sympathy.

"If just they just listened more, if no one but they could give more," said Orloff. "That is simply not the situation with a narcissist. It's so difficult for some empaths to accept that someone simply doesn't have empathy, and that they can't recuperate the other individual with their affection."

Narcissists love dramatization and confusion

Shannon Thomas, a specialist and writer of the book "Recuperating from Hidden Abuse," revealed to Business Insider that empaths buckle down for concordance, though narcissists are hoping to do the inverse. They appreciate disarray, and like to realize they can pull individuals' strings.

Narcissists control empaths by leading them on with discontinuous expectation. They will incorporate commendations and generosity into their conduct, causing their unfortunate casualty to accept that if they carry on in the right way, they will recover the loving individual who they once knew.

"Empathetic individuals tend to comprehend that we're all human, we as a whole have deformities, and they're willing to show restraint toward another person's self-awareness," Thomas said. "Empathetic individuals will be exceptionally patient if a narcissist says 'I truly need to transform, I know I'm not great.' They have these minutes where they kind of concede flaw, however they never really finish or trust it."

This is essentially a strategy narcissists use to reel their accomplice back in. With empaths, it is extremely powerful, because they need to help their accomplice and help them develop. At last, they are simply being abused further.

The empath can shape an injury bond

The push and draw nature of the narcissistic relationship can produce an injury bond between the person in question and the abuser, where it can feel practically difficult to leave the relationship, regardless of how much harm it is doing.

"With empathy comes the capacity and eagerness to take a gander at ourselves and take a gander at our very own flaws, and that gets exploited while the injury bond is going on," Thomas said. "It turns into a cycle for an empath who has been injury fortified because they start taking a gander at themselves, and what do they have to do to change, and what do they have to do different, and what their character defects are. It's the ideal set up, shockingly."

It very well may be difficult to grasp the reality you are in a narcissistic relationship from the outset, yet there are numerous warnings you can pay special mind to as you become more acquainted with one another better. Thomas said to protect yourself from narcissistic maltreatment, you ought to comprehend we are answerable for our very own development, and others are liable for theirs.

"When you meet individuals or are in relationships with them, you must be cautious that you're not doing their work, or needing their development more than they do," she said. "You need to perceive what they really improve."

Additionally, understand that limits are sound for all relationships. For empaths, limits can feel cruel, yet once they know about the quality of saying "no," they can shield themselves from individuals who are hoping to exploit them.

"Empaths don't need to turn out to be hard or remorseless to have the option to be sound," Thomas said. "It's imperative to perceive that not every person should be in our lives. We're going to run over individuals who we understand probably won't be sound for us, and you must approve of releasing them."

What is it about narcissists that is so powerfully alluring?

Like moths attracted to flares, us empaths appear to have an inclination for flying straight into perilous fellowships and soul-sucking relationships that leave us feeling depleted and unhinged. But then, again and again a large number of us fall into a similar snare, often missing the imperative life exercises being displayed.

Pretty much consistently Sol and I get messages asking about the dynamic among empaths and narcissists. Having been scorched by various different kinds of narcissists myself, I realize exactly that it is so natural to fall into the substantial gravitational draw of such individuals. Like dark openings, narcissists consume your feelings, physical wellbeing, and mental stability, significantly controlling and destroying your discernments and sensibilities.

Stirred Empath Book Advertisement picture

Can any anyone explain why empaths and narcissists – two oppositely contradicted kinds of individuals – feel a practically attractive draw towards one another? There are numerous speculations, yet at its core, I accept that it is Life's method for reestablishing harmony.

For instance, how about we inspect your run of the mill empath. Commonly empaths are profoundly minding, merciful individuals. The empath's motivation in life is to help recuperating in others, yet because of their serious affectability, empaths often battle to make sound limits for themselves, yielding to affliction, victimhood, codependency, and ceaseless selflessness. Presently, how about we inspect your average narcissist. Because of different injuries, center injuries and conditionings, narcissists hole up behind a glorified mental self-view which is communicated as being exceptionally enchanting and appealing, yet profoundly cutthroat, indifferent, conceited and coldblooded. Set up empaths and narcissists together? Both interact with their "transformed/invert" selves, and both are compelled to learn, develop and recuperate because of such an encounter (despite the fact that this doesn't generally happen promptly, however through experimentation). Be that as it may, it is significant for empaths to understand that they can never "mend" the narcissists in their lives – any type of recuperating must start inside narcissist's themselves.

CONCLUSION

The most significant approach to help an empath kid is to be as transparent with them as could reasonably be expected. They will consistently know when you are lying, so there is no reason for attempting to conceal things from them.

This doesn't mean spilling out the entirety of your issues to your kid. Recognize any issues suitably, yet disclose that you ready to deal with them and the youngster shouldn't be concerned.

You need to pass judgment on every youngster on an individual premise to work out the amount to let them know and what consolation to give. Be that as it may, you will know when you have it right because your youngster will unwind, grin more and be increasingly anxious to play and have a ton of fun.

Recall that your empath youngster is managing overpowering feelings that they are simply not experienced enough to adapt to. Be that as it may, tuning in to their feelings of dread, consoling them and giving them a lot of adoration and embraces will go far to helping them adapt to these feelings. It will likewise ensure they grow up realizing how to deal with their gift and use it successfully as grown-ups.

Lightning Source UK Ltd.
Milton Keynes UK
UKHW021425310521
384684UK00002B/517

9 781803 040493